AMERICA'S ODDEST
HOLIDAYS

By Erika Edwards

Gareth Stevens
PUBLISHING

Please visit our website, www.garethstevens.com. For a free color catalog of all our high-quality books, call toll free 1-800-542-2595 or fax 1-877-542-2596.

Cataloging-in-Publication Data

Edwards, Erika.
America's oddest holidays / by Erika Edwards.
p. cm. — (Weird America)
Includes index.
ISBN 978-1-4824-4019-5 (pbk.)
ISBN 978-1-4824-4020-1 (6-pack)
ISBN 978-1-4824-4021-8 (library binding)
1. Holidays — Juvenile literature. 2. Holidays — Miscellanea — Juvenile literature. I. Title.
GT3933.E39 2016
394.26—d23

First Edition

Published in 2016 by
Gareth Stevens Publishing
111 East 14th Street, Suite 349
New York, NY 10003

Copyright © 2016 Gareth Stevens Publishing

Designer: Sarah Liddell
Editor: Ryan Nagelhout

Photo credits: Cover, p. 1 (arrow) Mascha Tace/Shutterstock.com; cover, pp. 1 (main), 10, 11 Flickr upload bot/ Wikimedia Commons; sidebar used throughout zayats-and-zayats/Shutterstock.com; background texture used throughout multipear/Shutterstock.com; p. 5 bonchan/Shutterstock.com; p. 6 Dmitry Savin/Shutterstock.com; p. 7 Opusztaszer/Wikimedia Commons; p. 8 Khudoliy/Shutterstock.com; p. 9 Andre Carrotflower/ Wikimedia Commons; p. 13 Frank van Delft/Cultura/Getty Images; pp. 14, 29 (cobra) Eric Isselee/Shutterstock.com; p. 15 acceptphoto/Shutterstock.com; p. 16 Portland Press Herald/Contributor/Portland Press Herald/Getty Images; p. 17 Cyrus McCrimmon/Contributor/Denver Post/Getty Images; p. 19 Neelix/Wikimedia Commons; p. 21 Tomsickova Tatyana/Shutterstock.com; p. 22 Multichill/Wikimedia Commons; p. 23 Mangus Manske/Wikimedia Commons; p. 24 AVN Photo Lab/Shutterstock.com; p. 25 Fœ/Wikimedia Commons; p. 26 Andrew Gray/Wikimedia Commons; p. 27 Chelsea Lauren/Contributor/WireImage/Getty Images; p. 29 (bee) irin-k/Shutterstock.com; p. 29 (foot) Gwoeii/ Shutterstock.com; p. 29 (pig) Tsekhmister/Shutterstock.com; p. 29 (orange bubble wrap) Coprid/Shutterstock.com; p. 29 (clear bubble wrap) M88/Shutterstock.com; p. 29 (nothing sign) Vladislav Gurfinkel/Shutterstock.com.

Printed in the United States of America

CPSIA compliance information: Batch #CW16GS: For further information contact Gareth Stevens, New York, New York at 1-800-542-2595.

CONTENTS

Celebrating the Weird 4

What's a Dyngus? 6

Eeyore's Birthday Party 10

Dog Days at Work 12

Horses, of Course 14

A Day for Pie 16

Morning Ice Cream? 18

Lunch for Bears 20

Arggggg! 22

Tartan Day. 24

Hats and More Hats 26

Sandwiched Holidays 28

Glossary. 30

For More Information 31

Index 32

Words in the glossary appear in **bold** type the first time they are used in the text.

CELEBRATING THE WEIRD

Holidays are days of celebration. Here in America, there are so many well-known holiday celebrations like the Fourth of July and Thanksgiving. But did you know that pretty much any day can be a holiday?

Many different organizations and groups in America have interests that are very important to them. To celebrate, many of them **sponsor** holidays by continuing **traditions** or even creating them. Some even become recognized by the US government. So switch out St. Patrick's Day for Dyngus Day and Halloween for Eeyore's Birthday Party, and let's get to celebrating!

What Makes a Holiday Odd?

While some holidays that you'll read about have very respectable meanings or origins, like National Tartan Day, some of them are kind of silly, like Mad Hatter Day. What makes them odd or weird is that they aren't easily recognizable to many Americans!

November is considered
Peanut Butter Lovers Month.

5

WHAT'S A DYNGUS?

Dyngus Day, or Śmigus-Dyngus, is a holiday brought to America by Polish **immigrants**. Dyngus Day is celebrated the Monday after Easter, an important Christian holiday. It celebrates the end of Lent, the 40 days before Easter when many Christians give up certain things or stop eating meat on certain days.

In early Dyngus Day celebrations, people were splashed with water unless the splashers were given gifts, usually a decorated egg called a *pisanka*. The Śmigus tradition was for boys to lightly hit girls on their legs with small sticks or switches from trees called pussy willows. It was a way for a boy to show he liked a girl!

Dyeing Eggs

To make decorated eggs in the Polish tradition, you dip them in different-colored dyes. After dipping the eggs in the lightest dye, you cover areas you want to stay that color with wax. The wax protects the color when you dip the eggs into the next-darkest dye. You continue this way as you dip the eggs into darker and darker dyes.

Pussy willow branches are used because they're some of the first plants to bud in spring.

7

Dyngus Day in the United States is a bit different than in Poland. Buffalo, New York, is the unofficial Dyngus Day capital of America. The first Dyngus Day was celebrated there in the 1870s. Every year, Buffalo holds a Dyngus Day parade through the part of the city where Polish people first settled when they came to America. There are also celebrations in Pittsburgh, Pennsylvania; Cleveland, Ohio; South Bend, Indiana; Elizabeth, New Jersey; and Bristol, Connecticut.

Dyngus Day celebrations in the past would stretch into the Tuesday after Easter. This is when women would get back at men by splashing them with water and tapping them with pussy willows!

Kitten Willows?

Pussy willows got their name from an old Polish legend! One spring, baby kittens fell into a fast-moving river while chasing butterflies. The kittens' mother sat crying by the riverbank looking for them. The willows heard her crying and lowered their branches to save them! That's how they got their fuzzy buds—they're fuzzy like kittens!!

Today's Dyngus Day celebrations have both men and women splashing water and hitting each other with pussy willow branches on the Monday after Easter.

EEYORE'S BIRTHDAY PARTY

"Sad? Why should I be sad? It's my birthday. The happiest day of the year." These words, spoken by the donkey Eeyore to his friend Winnie-the-Pooh, couldn't be truer than they are in Austin, Texas, on the last Saturday in April.

Eeyore's Birthday Party was first put on as a small gathering of the English department at the University of Texas at Austin. Since then, it has grown into a daylong festival. It's now held by the Friends of the Forest Foundation and includes singing, dancing, drum circles, face painting, and costumes!

The Eeyore of Liberty is at Eeyore's Birthday Party every year, usually by the drum circles. What could be more odd and American than that?

A Good Cause

Even though Eeyore's Birthday Party is a time for fun and games, it also doubles as a fundraiser for local charities. This happened when the Friends of the Forest Foundation took over the party planning. Some of the charities that have received donations include the Boy Scouts of America, Hospice Austin, and, of course, Donkey Rescue.

egg toss at Eeyore's Birthday Party

DOG DAYS AT WORK

Have you ever wondered what it would be like to have dogs in school? What if your teacher was allowed to bring his or her pet into the classroom? That is exactly what Take Your Dog to Work Day is all about.

The holiday was created by Pet Sitters **International** in 1995 and takes place in June every year. The hope is that having man's best friend in the workplace will decrease anxiety, increase productivity, and create awareness for animal adoption. Take Your Dog to Work Day is also a really fun experience for the dogs because they get to hang out with some new friends and spend the day with their owners.

More Dog Holidays

Pets have lots of holidays. January 14 is National Dress Up Your Pet Day, where pet owners put their furry friends in their Sunday best. March 3 is one of the weirdest holidays on the calendar: If Pets Had Thumbs Day. People are supposed to imagine what it would be like if their pets had thumbs like people!

For at least one day a year, dogs don't have to wonder what their owners do once they pat them on the head and leave for work.

13

HORSES, OF COURSE

In 2005, March 1 was chosen as National Horse Protection Day. Pet lifestyle **expert** Colleen Paige was looking to spread awareness of the dangers facing unwanted horses in the United States.

Have you ever thought about getting a horse as a pet? One way to help is to adopt a horse in need. If you aren't in a position to adopt a horse, you can celebrate by offering to feed a neighbor's horse or maybe give it a bath. You could also plan a food drive or host an adoption event. You could even **foster** or sponsor a horse before it finds a forever home!

Do you have a horse in your neighborhood? Be sure to pay it a visit on March 1!

American Horses

It seems like horses have lived in America forever, but they're not **indigenous**! North American horses went extinct, or died out, around the same time as woolly mammoths! Spanish settlers brought the horses we know today to the Americas in 1519. Still, Americans celebrate December 13 as National Day of the Horse!

15

A DAY FOR PIE

Pumpkin pie for Thanksgiving is pretty normal. Apple pie might find its way to your Fourth of July picnic. But maybe one of the coolest and most underrated holidays in the United States is a day to celebrate all pies—January 23 is National Pie Day!

A schoolteacher named Charlie Papazian created National Pie Day in 1975, and the American Pie Council has sponsored the day since 1986. You can celebrate in many different ways: baking pies, having a pie-eating party, taking a pie to work, having a pie-throwing contest, and even passing along pie memories. So when January 23 rolls around, make sure to get baking—or just dig in!

pi symbol (π) pie

Two Pie Days?

There's also a second pie day! March 14 is considered Pi Day because the date (3/14) is the same as the first three digits in a **mathematical** number called pi (π). People also eat pies on Pi Day, but the American Pie Council stands behind the January 23 holiday. Why not celebrate both?

National Pie Day is a great day to hang out with Mom, Dad, or Grandma and whip up some tasty ways to celebrate!

17

MORNING ICE CREAM?

Have you ever gotten sick of eating cereal for breakfast? Oatmeal, bacon, and eggs don't interest you? In the 1960s, Florence Rappaport's six children were having the same thoughts in Rochester, New York. She decided to treat them to ice cream for breakfast as a way to celebrate the cold winter months. This is how National Ice Cream for Breakfast Day was born.

Since then, her children have grown up and spread the word about this "cool" holiday. Today, restaurants in the Rochester area offer special breakfast menus on the first Saturday of February to celebrate winter and make a cold day a bit colder—but a lot more fun!

Ice Cream for a Good Cause

Although National Ice Cream for Breakfast Day isn't the most serious of holidays, Florence Rappaport's family has used the holiday to raise money for charity each year. For several years, the money raised in the Rochester area went to the western New York chapter of the Make-A-Wish Foundation.

Experts think they have nailed down the year National Ice Cream for Breakfast Day started. In 1966, a huge snowstorm hit Rochester and closed schools. People think that's why Rappaport's kids were so bored!

maple bacon ice cream

19

LUNCH FOR BEARS

No matter where your favorite teddy bear is from, it should definitely join you on July 10 for Teddy Bear Picnic Day! The beginning of this holiday comes from a song called "Teddy Bears' Picnic," which was written by John W. Bratton. It wasn't until 1932 that lyrics were added by Irish songwriter James Kennedy.

The idea of an actual picnic was brought about by Royal Selangor in 1988. Today, the holiday is celebrated in national parks around the United States. Some activities in more recent celebrations include live performances of the song, lawn games, face painting, photos, and even goody bags!

Why Called Teddy?

Why are they called teddy bears? In 1902, President Theodore "Teddy" Roosevelt wasn't able to find a bear during a hunting trip. Guides found an old, hurt bear and tied it to a tree, but he refused to shoot it. The story spread, and a candy store started selling stuffed bears as "Teddy's bears."

Some kids take their teddy bears everywhere. Why not pack up your fuzzy best buddy and have a great time outside?

21

ARGGGGG!

From Captain Hook to Captain Jack Sparrow, pirates are daring, adventurous, and exciting. No wonder September 19 is International Talk Like a Pirate Day. One day in 1995, two friends—John Bauer and Mark Summers—were playing racquetball when one cheered the other on with the pirate's call of "Arggggg!" The two loved it so much that they decided to keep it up for the whole day.

In 2002, writer Dave Barry wrote about it in a national newspaper article. Since then, more and more people have chosen to celebrate this wacky, fun, and silly holiday. If you choose to celebrate, you'll have to practice saying words like "ahoy" and "avast!" so you get the lingo down for next September.

John Bauer and
Mark Summers

Donuts for Talk Like a Pirate Day

Since Barry mentioned the day and doughnut company Krispy Kreme together in the article, the company has jumped on the Talk Like a Pirate Day bandwagon. On September 19, all you have to do is talk like a pirate to get a free glazed donut. If you dress as a pirate AND speak like one, you can take home one dozen free donuts!

Even though it's cool to just change the way you talk, dressing like a pirate can help you get into the holiday spirit. Grab a pirate hat and maybe even a foam sword, and talk like a pirate!

23

TARTAN DAY

America is made of many different groups of people. Americans related to Scottish immigrants have their own holiday to celebrate Scottish **culture**. National Tartan Day takes place April 6 and is a day for Scottish Americans to wear their tartan patterns. Tartan is a pattern made of crossing horizontal and vertical lines and can be many different colors. Common colors are red, black, blue, green, and yellow. You might recognize these patterns from **kilts**.

The holiday was unofficially celebrated for many years before Scottish Americans worked to get it recognized by the government. By 2005, both houses of Congress had passed **resolutions** making it an official US holiday!

*traditional
Scottish tartan hat*

The US Senate passed Senate Resolution 155 in 1998, and the House of Representatives passed a companion bill—House Resolution 41—in 2005.

Why April 6?

National Tartan Day is celebrated on April 6 because that day is important to Scotland's history. In 1320, Scotland claimed its **sovereignty** against England's claim of Scottish territory with the signing of the Declaration of Arbroath. It's said that many of the ideas in the Declaration of Independence were **influenced** by the Scottish declaration.

25

HATS AND MORE HATS

In Lewis Carroll's *Alice in Wonderland*, the Mad Hatter, or the Hatter, is a strange character Alice meets and has a tea party with. The Hatter annoys and challenges Alice in the book, speaking in riddles or short comments and quickly switching seats around her.

In the sketches of *Alice in Wonderland* by illustrator John Tenniel, the Hatter also wears a hat that reads "In this style 10/6." The people who first celebrated Mad Hatter Day took the words "in this style" to mean to act silly, like the Mad Hatter acted in the book. They took the "10/6" to mean October 6, and so Mad Hatter Day was born!

John Tenniel's
Mad Hatter

Mad Hatter Day was first celebrated by a group of people in 1986 in Boulder, Colorado.

We're All a Little Mad

The Mad Hatter is a big part of pop culture. In the 1951 Disney cartoon, he was short and grey-haired. Actor Johnny Depp played the character in the 2010 movie *Alice in Wonderland* with red hair and lots of makeup. The Mad Hatter is also a character who fights Batman in comic books!

SANDWICHED HOLIDAYS

Whether it's ham and cheese or peanut butter and jelly, everyone has a favorite sandwich. Make sure to enjoy yours on November 3 because it's National Sandwich Day! Of course, National Sandwich Day is sandwiched between two other holidays: Deviled Egg Day is November 2, and King Tut Day is November 4!

The month of November is full of food holidays. Homemade Bread Day (November 17) is a few weeks too late to enjoy fresh homemade bread on National Sandwich Day, but there are plenty of other tasty days to enjoy. National Indian Pudding Day is November 13, and November 23 is Eat a Cranberry Day.

Every Day a Holiday!

Other fun, odd holidays celebrated in the United States include: Old Rock Day, Roller Coaster Day, Learn About Composting Day, and Ice Cream Sandwich Day. There's a holiday associated with pretty much every day on the calendar. So if you didn't find a new holiday you're crazy about, there are plenty more out there.

EVEN MORE ODD HOLIDAYS

FUDGE

July 10
Don't Step on
a Bee Day

June 2
Yell "Fudge" at Cobras
in North America Day

ON THIS SITE
IN 1897 NOTHING
HAPPENED.

January 16
National Nothing Day

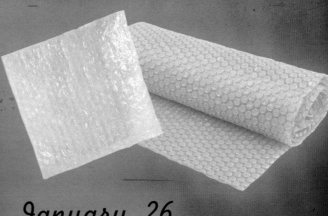

January 26
Bubble Wrap
Appreciation Day

March 1
National Pig Day

GLOSSARY

culture: the beliefs, practices, and ways of life of a group of people

expert: someone with great knowledge about a certain subject

foster: to provide a temporary home for

immigrant: someone who moves to a new country to settle there

indigenous: occurring naturally in a certain place

influence: to have an effect on

international: involving two or more countries

kilt: a knee-length skirt usually made of tartan worn by men in Scotland

mathematical: relating to numbers and math

resolution: a formal statement of feelings or wishes

sovereignty: freedom from outside control

sponsor: to pay for and offer support for something

tradition: a practice or way of thinking handed down from the past

FOR MORE INFORMATION

BOOKS

Lewis, J. Patrick. *World Rat Day: Poems About Real Holidays You've Never Heard Of.* Somerville, MA: Candlewick Press, 2013.

Weiss, Lynne. *United States: The Culture.* New York, NY: Crabtree Publishing, 2013.

WEBSITES

Days of the Year
daysoftheyear.com
Find many more American holidays listed here by date.

Holiday Insights: Bizarre, Wacky, and Unique Holidays
holidayinsights.com/moreholidays
Find the weirdest and wackiest holidays listed here.

National Tartan Day
tartanday.org
Learn more about National Tartan Day and the rich Scottish American culture in America.

INDEX

Alice in Wonderland 26, 27

American Pie Council 16

Austin, Texas 10

Bauer, John 22

Buffalo, New York 8

Carroll, Lewis 26

Deviled Egg Day 28

Dyngus Day 4, 6, 8, 9

Eat a Cranberry Day 28

Eeyore of Liberty 10

Eeyore's Birthday Party 4, 10, 11

Friends of the Forest Foundation
10, 11

Homemade Bread Day 28

International Talk Like a Pirate
Day 22, 23

King Tut Day 28

Mad Hatter 26, 27

Mad Hatter Day 4, 26, 27

National Horse Protection Day
14

National Ice Cream for Breakfast
Day 18, 19

National Indian Pudding Day 28

National Pie Day 16, 17

National Sandwich Day 28

National Tartan Day 4, 24, 25

Paige, Colleen 14

Papazian, Charlie 16

Peanut Butter Lovers Month 5

Pet Sitters International 12

Pi Day 16

Polish 6, 8, 9

pussy willows 6, 7, 8, 9

Rappaport, Florence 18, 19

Rochester, New York 18, 19

Selangar, Royal 20

Smigus-Dyngus 6

Summers, Mark 22

Take Your Dog to Work Day 12

Teddy Bear Picnic Day 20

Tenniel, John 26